Disguises for your Dog

by Lynn Chang

Disguises for

Thomas Dunne Books

St. Martin's Griffin

your DOG

by Lynn Chang

New York

THOMAS DUNNE BOOKS.
An imprint of St. Martin's Press.

www.stmartins.com

Library of Congress Cataloging-in-Publication Data

Chang, Lynn.
    Disguises for your dog / by Lynn Chang.—1st St. Martin's
Griffin ed.
        p.   cm.
    ISBN 0-312-26277-9
    1. Costume.   2. Dogs-Equipment and supplies.   I. Title.
TT633.C475   2000
745.5—dc21   00-034494
                                                         CIP

First St. Martin's Griffin Edition: October 2000

10 9 8 7 6 5 4 3 2 1

dedicated
to all
pets & pet owners everywhere

with special thanks to
Betsy, Melissa, Fox
and my cat, Sheefen

Table of Contents

INTRODUCTION

Introduction

I have always felt that dogs are an open book. Their readiness to please is always so transparent. Dogs are just unbearably happy just to be in your presence. This utter devotion is reflected everywhere: from the morning breath that pants the beginning of a new day to the thumping tail that greets you when you return from work. You are the apple of those bright shiny eyes.

Yet, deep down within every dog's heart is a hidden desire often overlooked. The desire to be mysterious, to be incognito, to live out their darkest fantasies. This book was written with this important need in mind.

Between these pages you will find simple and easy instructions to make outfits that should only be considered as a first step in self discovery for dogs around the world. Your dog will love you all the more for giving these disguises a go!

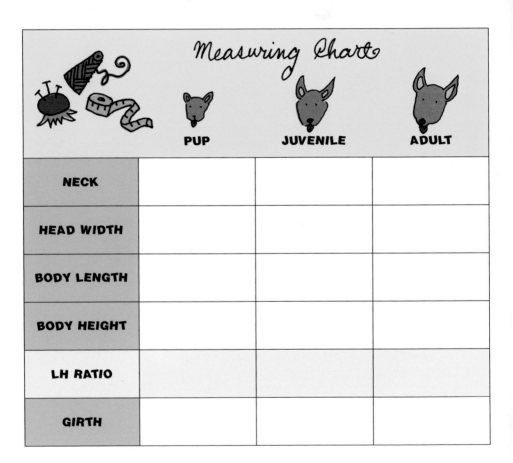

	PUP	JUVENILE	ADULT
NECK			
HEAD WIDTH			
BODY LENGTH			
BODY HEIGHT			
LH RATIO			
GIRTH			

Measuring Chart

Because dogs come in so many shapes and sizes, this measuring chart is
an absolute necessity. *Hint: Taking careful note of the body length/body
height ratio or "LH ratio" will save you many hours.*

THE GOLDEN MEASUREMENT RULE

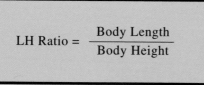

$$\text{LH Ratio} = \frac{\text{Body Length}}{\text{Body Height}}$$

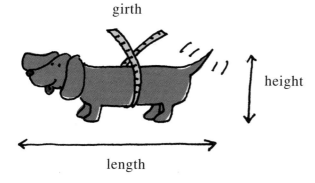

girth

height

length

Disguises for your Dog

FOX

Chapter 1

Enchanted
Dog

All the costumes in this chapter call for the generous use of sparkles.

Butter Dog

Float like a butterfly, sting like a bee.

THINGS YOU NEED

White Bristol Board
Tempera Paints
Elastic
Wire, Silver Balls
Sparkles

DIRECTIONS

1. Fold Bristol in two, cut out pattern and punch three holes along fold.

2. Using tempera paint, paint patterns on both sides of wings.

3. For special effect, draw patterns with white glue and sprinkle sparkles. Shake excess sprinkles off when dry.

4. Twist wire around dog collar and attach balls to wire ends.

5. Thread lengths of elastic through punched holes and tie around dog's midsection.

Fairy Dog Mother

May all your dreams come true

THINGS YOU NEED

Tulle
Tinfoil, Cardboard
Length of Pink Satin Riboon, Elastic
12" ¼" Diameter Wood Dowel
Silver Sparkles

DIRECTIONS

1. Cut out a rectangle of tulle. It should be 12" wide and twice your dog's girth.
2. Take white glue and draw a curly pattern on tulle and sprinkle with sparkles. When dry shake off excess sprinkles.
3. Form a casing as shown and thread satin ribbon through.
4. Cut a star out of cardboard. Cover star with tinfoil. Wrap dowel with tinfoil and attach star.
5. Cut out cardboard length with one serrated edge and cover carefully with tinfoil. Attach ends together to form crown. Place crown on dog's head.
6. Place tulle skirt around dog, tie ribbon in back. Put wand in dog's mouth.

You are My Sunshine Dog

April showers bring May flowers.

THINGS YOU NEED

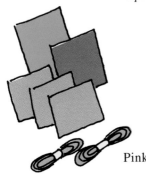

Purple Bristol Board
Purple Felt (3 squares)
Green Bristol Board
Green Felt (2 squares)
Pink and Green Embroidery Thread

DIRECTIONS

1. Cut out a circle in middle of the purple bristol board. It should be 1" wider than the diameter of your dog's neck.

2. Fold pink and purple pieces of felt in two a cut out petal shapes as shown.

3. Assemble petals around the board. Once satisfied, glue petals in place. Using pink embroidery thread blanket stitc around edges.

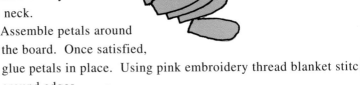

4. Cut two leaf shapes, glue onto green bristol, trim and finish edges

5. Place finished headpiece over dog's head. Simply stunning.

Chapter 2

the collar

The proper accesory helps everyone to stand taller, be more productive,
and feel better about oneself.

Spaghetti & Meatballs

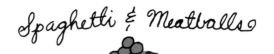

The secret is in the sauce.

THINGS YOU NEED

Adjustable "Collar"
Red Gingham Table Cloth (washable)
Mom's Sauce
Spaghetti
Colander
Grated Parmesan Cheese

DIRECTIONS

1. Boil salted water on stove. When water is boiling add spaghetti.
2. Meanwhile cut out a 12" x 12" square of the red gingham tablecloth.
3. Fold square in half and cut a 2" diameter circle.
4. Place dog's head through tablecloth making sure pattern is right side up.
5. Fasten collar securely on dog's head.
6. Remove pasta from stove and drain in colander. It should be perfectly al dente.
7. Stir sauce into pasta and carefully place in collar.
8. Add parmesan cheese to taste. Bon appétit!

Oriental Lamp

The perfect accent in any room.

THINGS YOU NEED

Adjustable "Collar"
18" Length of Silk Fringe
1 Yard of Fireproof Crushed Velvet
Standard 60 Watt Bulb
Electrical Components

DIRECTIONS

1. Lay collar flat. Coat with a thin film of white glue.
2. Place velvet fabric over collar pressing the fabric flat, making sure there are no bubbles. Wait 1 hour to dry.
3. Turn collar over and cut fabric ½" around edge of collar.
4. Place glue on fabric ends and fold over collar for a clean finish.
5. Taking a needle and thread, attach silk fringe to wide edge of velvet with tiny invisible stitches.
6. Assemble electrical components and fasten securely to collar.
7. Place collar on dog's head, plug in and turn on. For best effect, turn off all other room lighting.

The Flying Saucer

Close Encounters of the Canine Kind.

THINGS YOU NEED

Adjustable "Collar"
Tinfoil
Black and White Construction Paper
Cardboard
12" Length of
Red, White, and Blue Ribbon

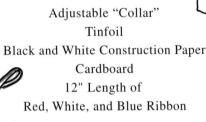

DIRECTIONS

1. Pull out a 2' length of tinfoil and spread a thin layer of white glue and place the collar on the foil.
2. Neatly fold foil edges inward.
3. Meanwhile cut out 7 1½" black circles and 7 1" white circles.
4. On white circles draw an oval face with large slanted black eyes as shown. Color face in green and paste onto black circle.
5. Glue circles around collar even distances apart.
6. Cut out a 2" medallion out of the construction paper. Print "USA Ambassador". Punch hole on top of medallion and thread ribbon through. Fasten around dog's neck.
7. Place collar on dog.

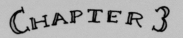

CHAPTER 3

Fun

with

Egg Cartons

One of the most underutilized
pieces of modern packaging:
Egg Cartons.
Instead of
recycling
them next time,
why not give one
of these suggestions a whirl
to lend them another useful life?

Finger Food Dog

Your dog will be the life of the party!

THINGS YOU NEED

1 Egg Carton*
Elastic
Hors D'oeuvres

DIRECTIONS

1. Thoroughly wash and dry egg carton.
2. Punch three holes on each side of egg carton.
3. Cut 3 pieces of elastic. They should be 1" longer than the girth of your dog. Knot one end, feed the unknotted end through the egg carton hole slip through the other end and knot. Repeat for all 3 lengths.
4. Slip egg carton tray on dog. Elastic should be tied firmly, but not as to make breathing uncomfortable.
5. Fill each egg cavity with your favorite finger snack.
6. Refill as necessary.

*Use a 6 or 12 carton depending on your dog's length.

Picasso Dog

An excellent outlet for artistic expression.

THINGS YOU NEED

1 Egg Carton*
Acrylic or Other Water Based Paint
Paint Brushes, various sizes
1 Black Beret, size small

DIRECTIONS

1. Thoroughly wash and dry egg carton.
2. Follow steps #2–4 for "Finger Food Dog". Again, make sure carton is secured snugly.
3. Fill each egg cavity with paint leaving at least one cavity for water and another for mixing/blending paint.

4. Place brushes in dog's mouth for easy access.
5. Place beret on dog's head.

Use a 6 or 12 carton depending on your dog's length.

The Germinator

An effective way to expedite your seedlings any time of the year.

THINGS YOU NEED

1 Egg Carton*
Elastic
Planting Mix (50% soil, 50% peat moss)
Seeds

DIRECTIONS

1. Thoroughly wash and dry egg carton.
2. Follow steps #2–4 for "Finger Food Dog".
3. Fill each egg cavity ¾ full with the potting mix.
4. Using fingers make indentations for seeds. Follow seed instructions for appropriate depth. Once seeds are placed, sprinkle remaining potting mix on top.
5. Sprinkle water so that soil is slightly damp. Repeat daily making sure not to overwater.
6. Once seedlings have germinated, transplant into your garden. You will find seedlings germinate surprisingly quickly due to the warmth your dog generates.

*Use a 6 or 12 carton depending on your dog's length.

Chapter 4

Working Dog

Dogs yearn to be helpful.
This chapter illustrates the many ways
you and your dog can work together
for chores and cheer!

Dogercise

A great way to stay fit.

THINGS YOU NEED

2 Small Velcro Target Boards
6 Small Velcro balls
Wide Elastic

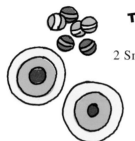

DIRECTIONS

1. Sew elastic into a sturdy loop that fits snugly around your dog's girth.

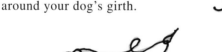

2. Sew velcro target boards onto elastic as shown.
3. Slip around dog's midsection, making sure the targets hang evenly when dog is moving. Adjust as necessary.

4. Once the target is in place, begin to throw velcro balls at target(s). There are countless creative ways to play. Devise your own rules for endless hours of fun!

Security Dog

You'll never feel safer.

THINGS YOU NEED

Small Flashing Light *(available at most hardware stores)*
Wide Black Elastic
Megaphone, Coat Hanger Wire
Cardboard
Glow in the Dark Tape

DIRECTIONS

1. Cut out a cardboard circle and write in bold letters: "House Protected by _____ (your dog's name)." Attach to collar.

2. Cut 4 lengths of glow in the dark tape and wrap each length around dog's feet.

3. Sew elastic into a band that fits snugly around your dog's girth and attach flashing light securely to elastic.

4. Taking wire, bend as shown into a megaphone fixture. Place around dog's neck and affix the megaphone.

5. Turn flashing light on. Your dog is ready to patrol.

Tidy Dog

Clean as a whistle.

THINGS YOU NEED

White Dust Cap, White Handkerchief
Lace Edging, Pink Ribbon
4 Small Wooden Scrub Brushes
Carpet Tacks, Wide Elastic
Feather Duster

DIRECTIONS

1. Sew lace edging to dust cap using tiny invisible stitches. Set aside.
2. Cut pink ribbon into two lengths. Tack ribbon to handkerchief forming an apron.

3. Cut elastic into five lengths. Use carpet tacks to attach elastic to scrub brushes.
4. Take fifth piece of elastic and sew into a small loop. Attach to feather duster as shown.
5. Tie apron around dog's waist, place cap on head, attach feather duster to tail and then place scrub brushes on feet. Sprinkle your favorite cleaner on any surface, dampen with water and place dog on top. Your work will be over before you know it!

CHAPTER 5

Classic Monsters

You and your dog will be guaranteed
to frighten the brave and chill the tenderhearted.
For Halloween or any time of the year.
Oooooooh Scary!

The Mummy

Terrifying!

THINGS YOU NEED

White Toilet Paper

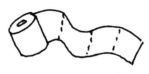

DIRECTIONS

1. Take one end of toilet paper and wrap around dog starting with tail, then back legs, torso, front legs and finally the head last. Be careful to overlap edges by approximately ½" for greatest effect.

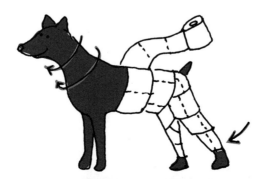

Dracudog

Frightening!

THINGS YOU NEED

1 Yard Black Fabric
Red Ribbon
Black Felt
Baby Powder
Flour Paste

DIRECTIONS

1. Cut off 2" length of fabric. Set aside and hem all edges of remaining piece of fabric.
2. Iron ½" of fabric strip on both sides.

3. Pin strip in place 6" from top edge of larger piece of fabric. Sew to form a casing and thread ribbon through.
4. Shirr fabric so it forms a collar as shown.

5. Cut out a 2" equilateral triangle from black felt.
6. For final assembly, powder dog's face lightly, tie on cape and glue felt triangle on dog's forehead. Super scary!

Frankendog

Frightening!

THINGS YOU NEED

Green Construction Paper
Black Construction Paper
Brown T-Shirt (chewed to rags)
2 Bolts

DIRECTIONS

1. Cut out a 3" wide length of green paper and cut out an equal length of black paper.

2. Glue black paper to green paper leaving 1" of black paper showing. Fringe black paper.

3. Draw stitches on green paper and form into a loop.

4. Cut a 1" width of green paper and attach bolts.

5. Place T-Shirt on dog and fit headpiece over dog's head.